THE TABLE

THE TABLE

DIANE VON FURSTENBERG

———

STYLED BY OLIVIER GELBSMANN

PHOTOGRAPHS BY STEWART O'SHIELDS

DESIGNED BY YOLANDA CUOMO

RANDOM HOUSE NEW YORK

Copyright © 1996 by Diane Von Furstenberg
Photographs copyright © 1996 by Stewart O'Shields
All rights reserved under International and Pan-American Copyright Conventions.
Published in the United States by Random House, Inc., New York, and simultaneously in Canada
by Random House of Canada Limited, Toronto.

Library of Congress Cataloging-in-Publication Data is available.

ISBN 0-679-44757-1

Associate Designer: Francesca Richer
Typesetting and composition: Robin Sherin

Random House website address: http://www.randomhouse.com/

Printed in Italy
24689753
First Edition

CONTENTS

INTRODUCTION

A HISTORY OF THE TABLE

To remove the table is to destroy the entire home:
it is to close the door on strangers, deny offerings to the gods,
condemn everyone to solitude, and jeopardize the most
humane acts of communion between man and man.
—Plutarch, *The Dinner of the Seven Wise Men*, A.D. 85

Throughout history and around the world, the table has been the center of home and social life. The bed and the bath are private retreats, while the table brings groups of people together. It is a symbol of warmth and community. Solitary meals can be taken on the run, off a tray, or in front of a book, but the table encourages socializing. The English word *companion* has a Latin root meaning "one who breaks bread with another." Families reconnect, executives clinch contracts, lovers flirt, and heads of state cement delicate alliances at the table. Births and weddings and other rites of passage are celebrated there.

The table's simple structure—upright supports for a flat surface, with space around the edges for human bodies—has adapted to different eras, places, peoples, and occasions. Western diners sit upright at formal meals, while those from Eastern cultures squat, sit, or kneel around a table built close to the floor. At elegant Japanese dinners, each guest is often provided with a table of his own, while their European and American counterparts usually call for a single expanse at which guests can converse side by side. Seating accessories for the table range from low unpadded stools to thronelike armchairs, or are dispensed with entirely in favor of cushions or the carpeted floor. The well-dressed Japanese table might display one lacquer bowl and a single perfect orchid; a nine-teenth-century French table garniture, on the other hand, typically weighted the table with more than fifty pounds of silver-gilt ornaments even before the many glasses, dishes, and utensils required for actual eating were added.

The origins of the table have been lost in time. Images of small, portable tables of wood or bamboo first appear in Egyptian wall paintings. The ancient Persians ate while reclining on couches next to small tables, a custom later adopted by many Greek city-states. The light three-legged tables that stood by Greek supper couches served as over-sized plates. Food was placed directly on their surfaces, and servants provided new courses for the meal by bringing in new tables. The elegantly groomed guests at Greek symposia (most of whom were male—women, except for courtesans, were rigorously excluded) enjoyed the pleasures of carefully planned food, wine, flowers, and music. The symposium's highlight, however, was its after-dinner conversation. From Socrates to Plato, Xenophon, Plutarch and beyond, Western civilization owes much of its philosophy to table talk.

Though their dining arrangements mimicked those of the Greeks, the Romans abandoned Hellenic restraint. At Roman tables the senses, not the intellect, reigned supreme. Wealthy hosts stimulated jaded appetites with rare delicacies and bizarre entertainments (one host is said to have amused diners with private gladiatorial battles, fought to the death). Dinner parties and dining rooms became ever more elaborate. The emperor Nero's dining room was a circular, ivory-paneled space that revolved constantly, set with a dome that opened to reveal the heavens and sprinkle flowers and perfume onto the diners below.

With the collapse of the Roman empire, the custom of private dinner parties given in rooms set aside only for dining disappeared for more than a thousand years. Medieval homes made few distinctions between rooms and drew few boundaries between private and public life. Dining tables made of boards and trestles could be set up anywhere in the house and stored when not in use; servants sat along one side of the table in full view of other guests, with special chairs and table linens marking the places of important diners. For all the grandeur of the medieval table, its crowded seating and minimal tableware make it seem chaotic to modern eyes. An illuminated page from the *Trés Riches Heures*, which shows the wealthy and powerful Duc du Berry at dinner, perfectly captures the contrasts of the medieval table. The Duc's table coverings are sumptuous, his few serving pieces costly, the robes of his retinue richly woven and colored—the scene is full of luxury. Yet amid the splendor a crowd of courtiers and servants jostle together over their meal, while small dogs play and sniff the crumbs scattered on the floor.

Succeeding centuries saw the development of heavier, less portable tables and the refinement of tableware. Utensils replaced fingers as eating tools and elaborate napkin foldings and table coverings were developed. During the Renaissance and Baroque eras the table and its ornaments took on a new importance in the planning of a meal. Feasts were spectacles more than social gatherings. One dinner, given in Bologna's Palazzo Vizzani in 1693, seated sixty-six diners around a vast circular table. Each place was set with a silver bowl and an elaborately folded napkin; in the table's center a sugar-paste sculpture—complete with grottoes, mythological figures, gilded griffins, and representations of the host's heraldic emblem, the palm tree—rose more than twenty feet high. Such tables took sculptors, painters, gilders, and other workmen hundreds of hours to assemble, but their dismantling was easy and cheap. Once the nobles withdrew after dinner, townspeople and servants were given free rein to consume the leftovers and loot the table decorations as they pleased.

The seventeenth century laid the groundwork for modern table settings and manners. In France, then the center of the civilized world, Cardinal Mazarin made the three-pronged fork fashionable and introduced the small round table, at which small groups could be seated without reference to precedence or rank. But it was the eighteenth century that saw the birth of a recognizably modern table. The Enlightenment's emphasis on the value, pleasure, and rights of the individual—as distinct from the status of the family or the power of the court—was reflected in homes designed for greater comfort and privacy. Though court protocol remained rigid, private dining customs expressed a new ease. Small tables designed just for eating, placed in private boudoirs or in rooms set aside only for dining, encouraged intimate meals. The classical ideal of the table as a place where like-minded friends could share conversation was reborn. Engravings from the era record not just state dinners but also intimate, candlelit rooms where one or two couples relax, free from the strain of formal etiquette. The eighteenth-century table was elegant and playful. Jean-François Bastide's novel *La Petite Maison*, published in 1752, tells of a nobleman who seduces a woman by showing her his luxurious home on the Seine. The highlight of the tour is the dining room, where a beautifully set table lowers as if by magic into the kitchen below, reappearing with clean dishes and fresh food at the beginning of each course. The woman is duly impressed—and the reader is left to imagine the pleasures possible in a room unwatched by servants' prying eyes.

Across the Atlantic, a brand-new nation was transforming European ideals and customs with new attitudes and optimism. International in sensibility, endlessly curious, and blessed with both elegance and common sense, Thomas Jefferson embodied the fledgling American spirit in both public and private life. He fostered the culinary variety that would become a hallmark of American tables by introducing new foods such as macaroni, French fries, vanilla flavoring, and ice cream. Rejecting English-inspired tables and furnishings, Jefferson brought Italian and classical styles to the New World and experimented with architectural innovations. Most important, his 1803 *Memorandum on the Rules of Etiquette* abolished European hierarchies of rank and class at American social and government gatherings, making the American table a meeting place of equals. Gathering the best from many lands and breaking the stranglehold of outmoded tradition, Jefferson helped establish the comfortable, eclectic, welcoming approach that marks American tables and entertaining today.

The table's progress toward a modern informality suffered a sharp setback during the nineteenth century. Caught in the midst of an industrial explosion, both the land-based aristocracy and the newly wealthy middle class found themselves battling for social distinction, and the nineteenth-century table epitomized the age. Dark and massive, it sat in a gloomy dining room (deep-toned walls and curtains were thought to act as the ideal foil to the white of table linens and the bright colors of food), which remained empty through most of the day. Bristling with newly invented dishes and utensils, from fish forks to celery boats, formal nineteenth-century dinner tables were glittering traps for the unwary. Manners were as complex and unforgiving as the place settings. Etiquette, one 1879 manual of manners said, is "the barrier which society draws around itself, a shield against the intrusion of the impertinent, the improper, and the vulgar." It's difficult to imagine an attitude more antithetical to the generous spirit of the table—and easy to understand why so many of the era's writers and diarists bemoaned the deadly artificiality of the Victorian dinner party.

Yet behind the scenes, the evolution of the modern table continued. Improvements in technology made a new variety of textiles, ceramics, and metalware widely affordable. Advances in transportation permitted the importation of objects from all over the world, making everything from Indian cotton tablecloths to Japanese blue-and-white porcelain bowls available to the imaginative host or hostess. Synthetic dyes created a bright new range of home furnishings, while the invention of gas and later electric illumination literally shed new light on the table. Efficient shipping and storage technologies widened the range of foodstuffs available to the cooks, permitting more varied and exotic menus than ever before.

The turn of the twentieth century ended the fussiness and constraint of the Victorian table forever. Two world wars demolished old social structures, the growing emancipation of women led to more simplified household arrangements, and an increasingly urbanized lifestyle necessitated a return to less formal and less space-consuming dining-room design. Pleasure and ease—rather than rigid rules—became the key influences on the table. By 1929 even the unswervingly traditional Emily Post could admit that "no rule of etiquette is less important than which fork we use." At the table a new era of comfort, generosity, and flexibility had dawned.

Contemporary American tables draw from the best of many cultures, styles, and eras. They combine the adaptability of medieval tables with eighteenth-century refinement and meld the conversational sparkle of a Greek banquet with the simplicity of a Japanese meal. They reflect styles of the past yet retain a sturdy Jeffersonian contempt for empty pomp. Personal style shapes the menus and decorations of today's best tables. They are eclectic, witty, and colorful. Above all, they are surprising: as alive, as unexpected, and as eternally new as modern life itself.

AN EXOTIC LUNCH

Muriel Brandolini is the wife of Count Nuno Brandolini d'Adda. She is half Vietnamese and half French/Venezuelan, and comes naturally to a passionate eclecticism. The backdrop for a quick Vietnamese lunch mixing business and pleasure in her New York apartment is a vast window framed by swooping magenta curtains. The table is draped with a ruby-red Turkish cloth, and guests sit at a banquette draped with antique silk sarongs or on Allegra Hicks chairs covered with a leopard-skin print. The dishes are blue-and-white Chinese porcelain and include an antique teapot and chopstick holders molded in a fish motif.

MI-SAO

———

(Serves six)

2 pork chops, cut into bite-sized pieces •tamari sauce for marinade
salt and pepper to taste • 1 lb. medium-sized shrimp, shelled and cleaned
1 tsp. crushed red pepper • 1 tsp. grated ginger • 1 tbs. lemon juice
3 tbs. sesame oil • 4 large garlic cloves, peeled and mashed
2 medium-sized red onions, chopped • 8 oz. dried Chinese yellow noodles
2 fresh jalapeño peppers, chopped • 1 ⅓ tbs. vegetable oil
2 medium zucchini • 2 carrots • 1 bunch asparagus • 1 head of broccoli
1 bunch of scallions • 1 head of cauliflower • 1 tomato
1 tsp. peanut oil • 1 bunch of fresh coriander, cleaned and chopped
1 tsp. mixed powdered spices (ginger, nutmeg, cloves, thyme, star anise)

Marinate the pork for 15 minutes in tamari sauce, adding salt and pepper to taste.
Marinate the shrimp in tamari sauce with the crushed red pepper, ginger, and lemon
juice. In a wok, heat 2 tbs. of sesame oil. Mix in garlic, onions, and pork, stirring until
golden, approximately 15 minutes. Remove and set aside. Boil noodles for 2 minutes.
Remove and drain, forming them into 6 pancake shapes. Fry the noodle pancakes in
1 tbs. sesame oil, until crisp and golden. Stir shrimp mixture and jalapeño peppers in
the wok in 1 tbs. vegetable oil on a very high flame for 1 minute. Remove and set aside.
Chop the vegetables (zucchini, carrots, asparagus, broccoli, scallions, cauliflower, and
tomato) into bite-sized pieces and stir into the wok with 1 tsp. of vegetable oil, 1 tsp.
of peanut oil, and 1 tsp. of tamari sauce. Sauté on a high flame until vegetables are
cooked but not mushy. Add pork and shrimp mixtures. Stir quickly, adding coriander
and spice mixture. Spoon onto noodle pancakes and serve.

RED BERRIES
AND CHAMPAGNE

Art and antiques dealer Louis Bofferding lives, works, and entertains in a classically proportioned townhouse on Manhattan's Upper East Side. His ever-changing collection of furniture and artwork floats in a neutral, light-splashed room, with the velvet upholstery of antique chairs providing the only touch of color. For an afternoon champagne party with friends, Bofferding arranges American brass chairs with buttoned leather seats around a 1950s Jansen table with blue steel legs and rubber wheels. The black lacquer surface is set with Fornasetti faux-malachite plates, eighteenth-century sterling flatware with green bone handles, and a cast-bronze elephant on a red-silk damask pedestal by Geoffrey Bennison. A turn-of-the-century Venetian glass chandelier hangs above the table, and the champagne is chilling on an eighteenth-century Italian console of gilded wood from the collection of Edward James. The Louis XVI armchair on the left is painted white and upholstered in antique Chanel mauve silk velvet. Belle Epoque painted side chairs sit in front of each window. The table on the right with the wooden top and brass legs is Meret Oppenheim's "Bird Table," circa 1939.

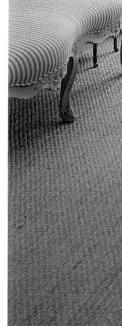

THREE-BERRIES DESSERT

———

1 box each fresh raspberries,
strawberries, and blackberries

Freshly squeezed juice of 2 oranges

1 tablespoon honey

¼ cup sugar

¼ cup fresh mint leaves, washed, dried,
and coarsely chopped

Wash and drain all the fruit and then hull the strawberries. Chill the berries in the refrigerator and then arrange them in a serving bowl. Whisk orange juice together with honey until well mixed, and spoon over fruit. Garnish with mint leaves and sprinkle with sugar. Serve with champagne and lace cookies.

FROM THE SEA TO THE CITY

The round table with black-and-white geometric patterns in the dining room of Marian McEvoy, editor of *Elle Décor* magazine, was painted by McEvoy herself. The neo-Gothic candelabra was found at a Paris flea market. She varies the color of the candles and the flowers around it with each dinner, although she admits to having a passion for red roses. The table sits in front of an elaborate fireplace designed by McEvoy. "I'm from California," she says, "and I always loved the sea and collected seashells. Since there is not much beach here I brought the sea to the city."

MARIAN'S TOMATO SOUP

—

5 pieces of oxtail

Several sprigs of fresh rosemary

5 whole cloves of garlic, peeled

1 yellow onion spiked with a dozen cloves

8 sweet red peppers, chopped

12 ripe plum tomatoes, chopped

6 carrots, chopped

½ pound small shrimp, peeled and deveined

sour cream

fresh dill

Bring two quarts of water to a boil in a large pot. Add the pieces of oxtail, rosemary, garlic, the onion, red peppers, plum tomatoes, and carrots. When the water returns to a boil, lower the heat and simmer for two hours. Remove oxtail bones. Working in batches, put entire mixture through a food processor or blender. Strain through a fine sieve. Put the soup back on low heat. Add salt and pepper to taste. Just before serving, throw in shrimp and let cook briefly. Serve with a dot of sour cream and a dash of fresh dill.

A GRAND LUNCH
BY THE SEA

Katharine Rayner serves a delightful Sunday lunch at her East Hampton home. Under the white awning that is pulled over the terrace to provide shade from the sun, you feel as if you've gone out to sea in a magnificent ship. The waves crash in the background, and a breeze ruffles the tablecloth. The entertaining is guaranteed to be equally sublime, since Rayner's friends are lively people from the media and the arts with lots to say. The furniture is from the porch of her childhood home in Atlanta. The flowers are all cut from her garden—a wonderful variety of roses, peonies, and purple salvia. The linens, in a seashell motif, were purchased at a local shop, while the glasses are from Biot, France. The plates are Italian, bought at The Cottage Garden in Atlanta. The menu includes a buisson d'écrevisses prepared by her French chef, Bernard Brule.

BUISSON D'ÉCREVISSES (CRAYFISH BUSH)

———

1 tablespoon ground pepper, white or black

8 bay leaves

12 sprigs of thyme

6–7 pounds live crayfish (generally delivered twice
weekly in season; ask your fish market)

5 lemons

7 bunches of parsley

mayonnaise

Boil three quarts of water in a large pot with the ground pepper, bay leaves, and thyme. While the water is coming to a boil, clean the first twelve crayfish, delicately removing the middle fin at the end of the tail (the intestine should come with it). Boil the crayfish for approximately 2 minutes, remove from water, and set aside to cool. Repeat until all crayfish are cleaned and cooked.

Wrap aluminum foil around a metal stand 5 to 6 times. Beginning from the bottom, arrange the crayfish on the stand, using toothpicks to support and hold them. Arrange a bed of parsley and lemons on a round tray, and set the stand of crayfish on it. Serve with mayonnaise.

INSPIRED BY MARIE ANTOINETTE

———

Susan Gutfreund is fascinated with table settings, and has a passion for the two arts involved, porcelain and textiles. For intimate luncheons and dinners in her New York apartment, she uses the room she calls the Wintergarden, from which she can watch the changing seasons in Central Park. She sets the table with a remarkable collection of objects. The porcelain is eighteenth-century Compagnie des Indes, originally made for a Swedish nobleman. She uses Swedish crystal to harmonize with the Swedish coat of arms on the dishes. The water glasses are Russian Jadite. The silver is a mixture of nineteenth-century French Odiot and eighteenth-century Meissen porcelain. The tablecloth is from her collection of old textiles.

Gutfreund's formal dining room has been decorated in blue and white, with striped fabric framed as panels lining the walls and a thinner stripe on the slipcovers of the chairs. The simplicity of this two-color theme gives a classic elegance to the room. The table is set with one of her favorite porcelains, the eighteenth-century Chantilly "oeillet." The crystal is Bohemian and engraved with hunting scenes, which is appropriate, since the hunting horn is the mark of Chantilly porcelain. The silver is nineteenth-century French by Odiot. For the centerpiece, instead of flowers, "I've used a Chantilly oil and vinegar container as a holder for nuts and candy," Gutfreund explains, "since it gives an opportunity for me to use another piece of porcelain."

TUNA FISH IN THE OFFICE

The garden designer Madison Cox works in a sunny loft in New York's Chelsea neighborhood. Cox plans gardens for rooftops, courtyards, and terraces in the city, and elsewhere he is commissioned for private estate gardens and public parks. The potted plants in the windowsills are samples for his clients. He sometimes has working lunches in the loft, in this case a hot tuna sandwich on grilled toast with a mesclun salad. The table is plated with stainless steel and the top is covered with leather. A trellis obelisk made for a garden party decoration sits near Wedgwood plates bought in a flea market in Paris.

DINNER AT SUNSET

I like to set the table of my hotel pied-à-terre in New York in an informal way. For a pre-theater meal I drape it with an antique silk sari and a plaid Balinese sarong. The room, designed by Jean-Paul Beaujard, reminds me of a room in a Russian novel. The blue glass candelabra with gilded cast-iron motifs are Russian. The carpet was specially ordered in Paris to look like a nineteenth-century design. The table and chairs are antiques from the French Empire period. The Orientalist paintings in their lavish gilded frames, the curtains of blue silk taffeta, and the view of the New York City skyline create a dramatic effect, yet with an intimate feeling. I love each of these fabulous objects by themselves, but they also look wonderful put together in this way.

The wonderful thing about potato and caviar is that it is so simple to prepare and so delicious to eat. Take a baking potato, wash it, and wrap it in foil. Let it bake at 375 degrees until cooked, about 45 minutes. Split the potato lengthwise and add a pat of butter, a tablespoon of sour cream, and a generous spoonful of caviar. Top it off with some chopped egg yolk and capers. The accompaniment is a watercress, beet, and walnut salad with a dressing of olive oil and lemon. The table is set with a collection of nineteenth-century English china from Bardith, Ltd. A Baccarat caviar holder sits inside the soupière.

A MILK-GLASS
COLLECTION

The home of Jacqueline Coumans, owner of the French fabric and upholstery shop Le Décor Français, is full of an eclectic collection of cherished objects; many are gifts from friends. There are lots of rich paisley fabrics that are sometimes thrown over the sofa or the ottoman or even used as curtain panels. They are her favorite things to collect because their colors are complex and mix with everything. In the living room, displayed on shelves against the white walls, is an assortment of milk-glass pieces collected during trips to flea markets. Milk glass is a product of the Depression in America, when porcelain was too expensive for most people. Jacqueline displays it on shelves and also uses it for evening buffets. The glass-top Jansen table with gilded bronze legs is from the forties. A pair of gilded metal Italian candelabra from the fifties frames the milk glass on the table.

FINGER-FOOD BUFFET

———

Moroccan spiced crab cakes
with cumin vinaigrette

Tuna sashimi on crispy flatbread
with salmon roe and chives

Smoked salmon on chickpea pancakes,
with yogurt tahini sauce

Moroccan spiced olives

Spanish cheeses with fresh fruit

Crudités with herb crème fraîche

Sesame bread sticks

Pepper bread sticks

CHEZ C.Z.

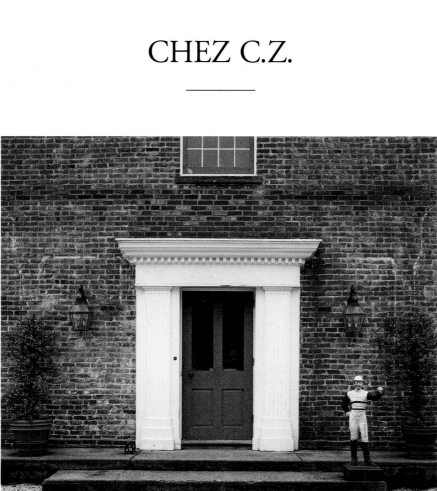

C. Z. Guest, a lifelong lover of gardens—which she designs, maintains, cherishes, writes about, and develops products for—is a classic American blend of sophistication and simplicity. She welcomes guests in a doorway painted chocolate and primrose, the riding colors of her late husband, and leads them through rooms filled with treasures and memories into the gardens beyond. In a blue-and-white salon, an octagonal Chippendale table holds a vase of white Dendrobium orchids.

A rare Louis XIII trictrac table (opposite), flanked by two Louis XIV armchairs, sits below a sixteenth-century primitive Dutch painting. Outside, one strolls through a brick-walled rose garden to the topiary garden designed by Guest's friend Russell Page, and then through a wildflower garden. The statue of the woman with the garlands was given by Henry Phipps to his daughter (Guest's mother-in-law) in 1910. It was made in 1710 by the French sculptor Coysevox. The original, from which three casts were made, is at Versailles.

Lunch is served under a trellised patio by the pool and tennis court (see following pages). The garden furniture was designed by C. Z. Guest herself. The flowers around the patio are her favorites: Vanda orchids, jasmine, passion flowers, and roses. She likes to prepare a buffet table and let guests help themselves at their leisure. On this occasion it is a feast of fresh summer foods, most just picked from her garden.

A GARDENER'S LUNCH

—

Steamed fresh baby sweet corn with hot butter

Fresh cantaloupe

Sliced red and yellow tomatoes with chopped onion and parsley

Turkey sandwiches on toasted country bread

Iced tea

Red and white wine

AN ARTIST'S TOWNHOUSE IN TRIBECA

French artist Arman has designed a limited collection of sculptured furniture, including this round glass-topped table with a bronze base in the shape of cello necks. The bronze armchairs are also cello-shaped. The candelabra, a cluster of sliced and then welded bronze violins, is another of the artist's works, as is the table's centerpiece, "As in the Sink," an "accumulation" of a white porcelain tea set. Portraits of Arman hang over three antique Japanese helmets on an inlaid Oriental cabinet. Corice, Arman's wife, enjoys entertaining in this harmonious space filled with Asian, African, and contemporary American art. For dessert on this occasion she has prepared pears poached in red wine with a raspberry purée and pistachio nuts.

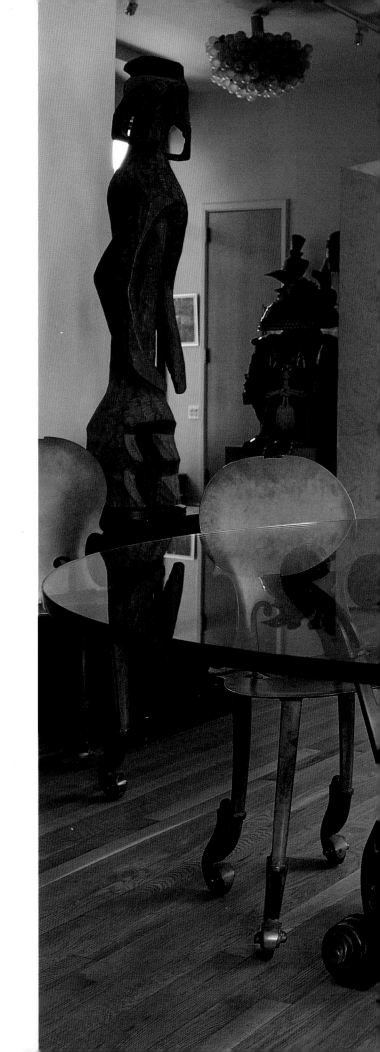

POACHED PEARS IN WINE

———

For the pears:
3 cups water • 1 ½ cups sugar
2 bay leaves • 6 red peppercorns • ½ cup red wine
4 firm Bosc pears

For the sauce:
2 cups fresh or frozen raspberries
½ cup lemon juice
⅓ cup sugar
1 cup pistachio nuts, finely chopped

Boil the water and sugar to make a syrup. Add the bay leaves and peppercorns, then the red wine. Add the pears to the syrup and cook for about 30 minutes, depending on the firmness of the pears.

To make the sauce, mix the raspberries and the lemon juice in a blender. Cook this mixture over medium heat for 10 minutes, slowly adding the sugar. Strain. Spoon sauce over poached pears, adding chopped nuts for garnish.

A COFFEE BREAK

Carlos Aparicio, a Cuban-born architect and interior designer, created his office in a gutted space that had been a storage room. His drafting room is next door. The office contains a mixture of twentieth-century furniture styles. The table is 1930s American, and the chairs are turn-of-the-century Viennese. Ready for a coffee break is a 1940s Spanish silver tray with a 1950s coffeepot—found in a flea market in Brazil—along with a creamer, sugar bowl, and glass mug, all by Boda. A Nigerian drum used as an end table sits near a 1940s French chair upholstered in mint velvet.

AT JANE'S

Co-founder of *Rolling Stone* magazine and the mother of three boys, Jane Wenner combines elegance and bohemia in a unique way. The atmosphere of her New York apartment is both refined and completely comfortable. At a long Welsh farm table in the kitchen, where the walls are covered with their drawings, the children enjoy a lunch of chicken fajitas and guacamole. In the formal dining room on the next page, the adults are served pork tenderloin in a shiitake ginger broth on a round English table surrounded by Anglo-Indian chairs.

SHIITAKE GINGER BROTH WITH PORK TENDERLOIN

———

Meat:
2 tablespoons hoisin sauce
2 tablespoons soy sauce • 2 tablespoons honey
1 pound pork tenderloin

Broth:
2 tablespoons fresh ginger, chopped
1 pound shiitake mushrooms, sliced very thin
1 bunch scallions • 2 teaspoons sesame oil • 6 cups chicken broth
1 tablespoon soy sauce • salt and pepper to taste
2 bunches watercress (stems removed) • ½ pound mung bean sprouts
2 cups Japanese soba noodles, cooked

Hot sauce:
Combine 2 tablespoons red chili paste,
½ cup rice vinegar, 1 teaspoon salt, and 1 tablespoon sugar.

Mix hoisin sauce, soy sauce, and honey. Pour over pork tenderloin and marinate for at least 2 hours. Grill tenderloin on outside grill or indoor broiler, basting with hoisin-soy-honey mixture every few minutes, until pork is dark and crispy.

Sauté ginger, shiitake mushrooms, and scallions in sesame oil for 1 minute on high heat. Add chicken broth, soy sauce, and salt and pepper. Let simmer 30 minutes. In soup dishes, arrange watercress, bean sprouts, noodles, and sliced roast pork. Ladle hot broth over the top and serve with hot sauce.

INSALATA CAPRESE

The art collector and dealer Barry Friedman and his wife, Patricia Pastor, entertain in an "undecorated" atmosphere where the intrinsic qualities of the art and furniture speak for themselves. The dining-room set is French Art Deco, made on commission for a client by Paul Follot in 1928. The photographs on either side of the window, each of which is made up of nine panels, are by the Guatemalan photographer Luis Palma. The wooden and iron sideboard is French, circa 1940, a collaboration by J. J. Adnet and Gilbert Poillerat. The floor lamp is from the late 1920s.

Patricia Pastor has set hand-painted porcelain plates from Tiffany's private collection atop glass chargers. The wineglasses are Tiffany's as well, but the other glassware, all gold-leafed, is a mix of things she has picked up on various trips to Italy to replace those relinquished to parties gone by. The sculptural flatware was designed by Jens Quistgardin in 1959. The candelabra are by Poillerat, circa 1940. Pastor has prepared insalata caprese as an appetizer: an arrangement of sliced ripe tomatoes, fresh mozzarella, and fresh basil leaves, drizzled with virgin olive oil and sprinkled with salt and pepper. It is served with sourdough Italian bread and a bottle of red wine.

CLOUDWALK FARM

On a hot and hazy day at my farm in Connecticut, I chose the shade of the oak trees beside the apple orchard to host a comfortable lunch. One of the pleasures of having a large garden is that you can choose a section to eat in depending on the season and what is blooming. I move the locale of the table according to whether I'm having a family lunch or something more elaborate, and sometimes entertain in surprising places. The blue hydrangeas set the tone on this day. A white antique embroidered tablecloth adds a note of freshness, its cross-stitched flowers bright against the deep green of the grass and trees. The chairs and the bench are antique Swedish furniture. The menu is a seasonal one, reflecting the fresh colors and tastes of the summer.

LEMON MERINGUE PIE

———

Pie Crust: 1 ½ cups all-purpose flour • pinch of salt
½ cup (1 stick) cold unsalted butter, cut into small pieces • ¼ cup ice water

Filling: 1 ¼ cups sugar • ½ cup flour • ¼ cup cornstarch
pinch of salt • 1 ½ cups water • 5 egg yolks • 2 tablespoons grated lemon peel
½ cup lemon juice • 4 tablespoons unsalted butter

Meringue: 8 to 12 egg whites
½ teaspoon cream of tartar • ½ teaspoon vanilla extract
pinch of salt • 6 tablespoons sugar

Preheat the oven to 350 degrees. Combine the flour and salt in a bowl and mix well. Using a pastry blender, two dinner knives, or your fingertips, cut the butter into the dry ingredients as quickly as possible, until the mixture resembles coarse bread crumbs. Sprinkle 1/4 of the ice water over the mixture and combine with a fork or your fingertips just until the dough holds together. If the dough seems too crumbly, add more ice water, 1 tablespoon at a time. Turn the mixture onto a sheet of waxed paper, gather into a ball, and press into a thick flat disk about 5 inches in diameter. Bring the paper around to enclose the dough and refrigerate for about 15 minutes to "relax" the dough for a more tender crust. Roll out the dough on a floured surface and fit into a nine-inch pie pan.

In the top of a double boiler over simmering water, combine sugar, flour, cornstarch, salt, and water. Cook 10 minutes or until the mixture thickens. Remove from heat, beat in egg yolks, one at a time. Return to heat; cook 6 minutes, stirring constantly, until thick and smooth. Add grated lemon peel. Remove from heat, stir in lemon juice and butter. Set aside.

To make the meringue, beat egg whites until fluffy. Add cream of tartar, vanilla, and salt. Continue beating, adding 1 tablespoon of sugar every minute. Beat until stiff peaks are formed, 7 to 8 minutes. Pour the filling into the pie shell. Spoon the meringue over the filling. Mound in peaks, covering the filling completely. Bake 15 minutes or until peaks are golden brown.

It is my family's custom to have Sunday lunch by the pool in good weather. The pool itself was designed in the 1930s. We sit on a roofed-in terrace on a Louis Philippe iron-and-wood bench and chairs. The food is set out on a cast-iron trolley. The tablecloth is printed with a colorful Oriental motif. This is a comfortable place where my friends, children, and dogs gather to eat, drink, and share laughs. On this day we had stuffed artichokes, spinach quiche, and blueberry pie.

A PEACEFUL COUNTRY RETREAT

Photographer Eric Boman and artist Peter Schlesinger share this Long Island country retreat. The dining room was part of an addition to the house made in the 1860s. The Ambrose Heal refectory table and collection of French 1870s "Henry IV" dining chairs sit on a Turkish kilim. The china is Chamberlain Worcester, circa 1840, set on Wedgwood creamware, circa 1975. The molded water glasses and wineglasses are American. The silver is nineteenth-century English. There is a Danish water jug and wine carafe from Boman's grandmother's ancestral home. The roses from the garden are held in an English celery glass, the napkins are from Williams Sonoma.

GREEN-PEA RISOTTO

(Serves four)

2 pounds fresh peas in their pods

4 cups chicken stock, preferably homemade

2 teaspoons olive oil

1 large yellow onion

2 cups short-grain Italian rice (arborio)

Salt and freshly ground black pepper

Fresh basil, about 25 leaves, chopped

4 teaspoons freshly grated Parmesan cheese (optional)

1 teaspoon butter (optional)

Rinse the pea pods and shell, reserving both peas and pods separately. Juice the pods in a vegetable juicer and reserve, or mix the pods in a blender with some of the stock, sieve, and reserve. Simmer the peas in the remaining stock, about 6 minutes. With a slotted spoon, return them to a bowl. Keep the stock hot on lowest setting.

In a pressure cooker, heat the oil over medium heat; chop the onion evenly and add to the oil, cooking until transparent and lightly golden. Add the rice and heat thoroughly (turn up heat) while stirring. Add the hot stock, all at once. Stir briefly to mix, and cover the pressure cooker. Leave it on high. When the pressure gauge reaches the correct level for grains (consult your manufacturer's manual), turn down the heat to maintain this level for 4 minutes. Remove the cooker from the stove and place it in the sink; run cold water along the edge of the lid (to stop the cooking) until the pressure valve has fully descended. Open and stir. The risotto may appear too liquid. Test the rice by biting into a few grains; if they are at all chalky in the center, you need to return the pot to the stove and cook the risotto a few minutes more, over medium heat, while stirring. Test again. By the time the rice is done to the right consistency (firm but cooked), the excess liquid will be absorbed.

Add the peas and the pod juice, and salt and pepper to taste. Add the chopped basil and, if desired, the Parmesan (this will melt and thicken the risotto). Finish with the butter, if desired, and serve as hot as possible.

PORCELAIN OBSESSION

The art dealer Khalil Rizk has put together a unique collection of crystal, silverware, and rare Chinese porcelain, and his dining room illustrates his conviction that these great objects from the past, which were made to be used, should not be left in a glass case. The table is graced with a set of four George III silver candlesticks, circa 1780. The flatware is from the same period. The plates are Chinese, made for export to various noble European families in the early eighteenth century. The table is set with two types of crystal: Baccarat and nineteenth-century amber-colored Bohemian.

When the rare pieces from Rizk's collection are gathered together, they bring harmony to the table. His dinner guests feel embraced by the generosity of their host, who shares with them his sense of elegance and love of art. A set of Louis XVI dining chairs by Arisse surround the table.

Chinese Export armorial plates hang on the walls of Rizk's dining room. The top plate was part of a service made for Empress Elizabeth of Russia in the middle of the eighteenth century. All these carefully selected objects, including the Georgian Irish silver tureen, are functional, with the exception of the porcelain figurine Turks, made by Meissen, which provide charming decoration.

MOROCCAN MINT TEA

Frederic Fekkai, the hairstylist who makes the rich and beautiful even more beautiful, entertains lavishly in the yard of his East Hampton beach house. In the summer, he gives exotic parties in an opulent Berber tent, which suits his personality. The objects here, which were collected from Sam's Souk in Manhattan, include a small cedarwood table carved in a mouchrabieh design, a traditional pattern used in Moroccan palaces. When two screens of this pattern are set beside each other, they create a one-way window. The hand-washer on the side table is useful, since no utensils are used in traditional Moroccan dining. After the meal, rose water is sprayed on the hands.

The cedarwood table above is carved and painted by hand in an Islamic design. The motif represents the earth and nature, the earth being the center circle and the surrounding carvings representing nature growing around it. The ceramic plates are all painted with natural plant dyes: the blue is cobalt, the red from the henna plant. The bread warmer on the side table was used by the Sephardic Jews in Morocco for Shabbat meals. It is made of a combination of zinc, brass, and copper. The Berbers, natives of the Atlas Mountains, would invest in such white metal pieces and then trade them for other items when needed.

CLEMENTE MEETS SCHNABEL

———

Francesco Clemente works in a serene studio on lower Broadway in Manhattan, where his own paintings sit beside the works of his friend the painter and sculptor Julian Schnabel. A few years ago Schnabel made a table for Clemente. It consists of sixteen tiles created from ceramic fragments and bronze grids filled with plaster. The many coats of plaster and different dyes make each tile seem like a painting of its own. The table legs are made out of the bronze left-overs from casting. Guests sit around this table on bronze benches with a webbing of burlap for the seats. Next to the table, watching over it, is a large Schnabel sculpture made of cast aluminum, welded steel, and cast-iron called *Capital with Bowls*. The painting on the floor behind the table is Clemente's *The Muse*. The artist usually eats alone here with his bowl of rice, like a monk.

MANHATTAN WITH AN
ITALIAN FLAVOR

———————

The jewelry designer, stylist, and photographer Marina Schiano likes to give small dinner parties with simple vegetarian dishes that draw on her Neapolitan heritage. Schiano has a great sense of humor and enormous vitality. She can have vivid conversations on the phone in any of four languages and prepare the most delicious pasta at the same time. She plans carefully, but the execution seems spontaneous. Schiano's dining table and the chairs and lamp behind it were all designed by Paul T. Frankl in the late twenties. Frankl was a great cabinetmaker known for "skyscraper" furniture. His book *New Dimension* was dedicated to his friend Frank Lloyd Wright. The candelabras are Venetian glass from the thirties. The dishes, which Schiano bought in Paris, were hand-painted in five different colors in a Japanese style at the turn of the century. The flute champagne glasses are from the Pottery Barn.

PENNE POMODORO

——

(Serves four)

4 tablespoons olive oil

4 cloves garlic, peeled and left whole

12 fresh ripe tomatoes, Israeli or plum

½ teaspoon (or to taste) peperoncino or red-pepper flakes

1 pound penne or rigatoni pasta

fresh basil

¼ pound Parmesan cheese, freshly grated

Heat the oil and the garlic cloves in a skillet for a few minutes. Remove the cloves before they turn brown (use just to flavor the oil). Add the ripe tomatoes whole and let cook for about 30 to 45 minutes. While they are cooking, add salt and peperoncino to taste. Remove the skins once the tomatoes are cooked. The resulting sauce should be chunky. Meanwhile, boil lots of water to cook the pasta. Add a handful of salt to the water and throw in the penne and cook for 12 to 14 minutes, until al dente. Drain the penne, return it to the pot, add the sauce, and cook for 5 to 10 minutes. Pour the penne into the serving bowl, add some fresh basil leaves, and serve with Parmesan cheese.

HOMAGE TO ELSIE DE WOLFE

Jane Stubbs's charming gallery and bookshop is situated in a picturesque townhouse just off one of New York's busiest avenues on the Upper East Side. Go down three steps, walk through a green door, and one seems to have arrived in an early-twentieth-century literary salon. Stubbs hosts frequent champagne parties and evening buffets in honor of new books or to celebrate exhibitions of art at the gallery on her second floor. Whether as part of a large gathering or a more private, intimate party, guests circulate in a cozy milieu created by the eclectic collection of prints and books and architectural drawings.

Jane Stubbs has prepared a table for six in honor of Elsie de Wolfe, who was renowned for her decorating and entertaining style. She has layered the table with three lavish antique fabrics reminiscent of the gold lamé that de Wolfe used for a tablecloth. The table itself is decorated with antique silver candlesticks wrapped with strings of pearls, rock crystals, and seashells. The silver elephants are from Cambodia. The coral branches are made of Venetian glass. The silver julep cups are family heirlooms. The plates are her great-grandmother's Wedgwood.

TEA CEREMONY
IN A TOWNHOUSE

———

The living room of interior designer Larry Laslo marries styles ranging from Queen Anne to Art Deco. The table with the glass top and bronze base was designed by Giacometti in the 1940s. Next to it sits a 1960s Lucite bench with a tiger-patterned velvet cushion and giant raffia tassels. The crystal chandelier is antique Waterford. The portrait above the mantel is by the French painter Jean Dupas, circa 1930. On the table are dishes purchased by Laslo in Kyoto, where he often works. They are what is known as Grand Pottery, all signed pieces by master craftsmen, who are National Treasures in Japan. Laslo's collection is mismatched, with some gold- and silver-leafed pottery and some lacquered bamboo, the perfect backdrop for the delicate cakes in an impromptu tea ceremony. Laslo adds his own style and touch of humor to the formality of the ceremony by serving hot sake and martinis along with the tea.

Laslo serves sweets and green tea from the New York branch of Toraya, a teahouse with a venerable heritage. The tea is prepared very carefully by gradually adding the hot water and mixing it with a special bamboo whisk. The wagashi, a delight to the eye and palate, are sweet delicacies, the preparation of which are an art form in Kyoto. They are traditionally served to guests on special occasions or given as gifts. They express friendship and goodwill, wishes for health and prosperity, and, above all, a desire for harmony.

CUISINE MINCEUR

———

Ann Barish likes to entertain both friends and celebrities at informal lunches in the several homes she and her husband keep. Keith Barish is the chairman of Planet Hollywood, and Ann aids in public relations, greeting and entertaining celebrities at the various Planet Hollywoods around the world. In New York they dine on a Prince of Wales table from the late 1800s, made in America. It was bought from an antique dealer in Aiken, South Carolina. The wallpaper in the dining room is antique Chinese, from Charles R. Gracie and Sons in New York City. The silverware is from Tiffany's and the china from Goode's in London. One of Ann Barish's favorite luncheon recipes is a Chinese chicken salad that is delicious and filling but not fattening.

CHINESE CHICKEN SALAD

(Serves four)

Dressing:
⅓ cup rice vinegar • 2 tablespoons dark sesame oil
1 tablespoon low-sodium soy sauce
½ cup thawed pineapple juice concentrate
¼ teaspoon ground ginger • ½ teaspoon minced garlic

Salad:
6 ounces skinned chicken breasts, boned with fat removed
4 cups shredded cabbage • 3 cups sliced mushrooms
1 cup chopped green onions
1 cup bean sprouts • 16 snow peas
½ cup julienned water chestnuts • 12 cabbage leaves

Combine the ingredients for the dressing and mix well in a blender. Cut the chicken into very thin strips. In a small nonstick pan, over medium heat, sauté the chicken until it is lightly browned, about 4 minutes. Mix shredded cabbage, mushrooms, green onions, bean sprouts, snow peas, and water chestnuts in a large bowl. Place 3 cabbage leaves on each plate. Arrange salad in 4 equal portions on cabbage leaves. Top with chicken strips. Drizzle 3 teaspoons dressing over each salad.

A DESIGNER'S EYE

Interior decorators Stephen Sills and James Huniford entertain in a whimsical Westchester guesthouse with a fireplace. The ceiling is painted in a faux Renaissance style. The mahogany Directoire wine-tasting table, which belonged to Christian Dior, is set with a pair of terra-cotta Wedgwood bottles, nineteenth-century Venetian glasses, Russian dessert plates decorated with thistles, and an eighteenth-century French vermeil service. A French coffee service from the 1940s sits on a twentieth-century Viennese side table.

LIKE A BIRD'S NEST

The terrace of Heather Cohane's Manhattan apartment is chockablock with flowers and trees in the summer: lilac, crab apple, maple, and hibiscus trees, jasmine, stephanotis, and gardenias that have spent the winter in a small attached greenhouse. Cohane was born in England, but when she married she moved into a beautiful Georgian house with a two-acre walled garden in southern Ireland. She hasn't been able to bear the idea of living without a garden ever since. When she came to New York, she was lucky enough to find a small penthouse apartment with a terrace facing south. Climbing clematis, grape vines, wisteria, and roses intermingle on white trellises in front of brick-red walls. There are large earthenware pots of various sizes brimming over with wild strawberries, herbs, lavender, and many varieties of roses. Cohane entertains in the evening with the awning down and lots of candles. The gilded glass dining table and the chairs come from Italy. The statuary comes from London, and the silver was inherited from her grandmother.

ENGLISH SUMMER PUDDING

———

2 pounds mixed soft fruit as available:
raspberries, blueberries, cherries, strawberries, blackberries

4 ounces sugar

8–10 slices of day-old white bread, without crusts

1 cup black currant or raspberry juice

Reserve ½ cup fruit and place the remainder in a large pan along with the sugar and 2 tablespoons of water. Simmer until the sugar melts and juices begin to run, approximately 3 minutes. Line a 2-pint pudding basin or soufflé dish with bread, reserving two to three slices for topping. Spoon the juices evenly over the bread, reserving 2 tablespoons, then add fruit. Cover the remaining bread and place a small plate on top. Add a weight (a can of food will do) to press the plate down. Chill the pudding overnight. The following day, turn the pudding out of its dish and use the remaining mixed-fruit juice and the black currant or raspberry juice to paint any white patches. Decorate with the reserved berries.

KENTUCKY COOKING

Charles Patteson, a Southern gentleman living in New York, cooks, sleeps, and entertains in one grand room that is furnished with hand-me-downs from his Kentucky family. The dining table is a Pembroke drop-leaf that can also be used as a side table when the leaves are folded. A Victorian secretary is used as a china cabinet. The table setting features Sheffield candlesticks, antique glassware, Royal Crown Derby serving plates, and old-fashioned silver mugs traditionally used for serving mint juleps during the Kentucky Derby. Patteson is a passionate cook, and gives intimate dinners using recipes from *Charles Patteson's Kentucky Cooking*.

MINT JULEPS

———

12 julep cups or heavy 10-ounce glasses

crushed ice

3 cups granulated sugar

1 ½ cups water

mint sprigs

24 ounces of 100-proof bourbon

Place the cups or glasses in the freezer for several hours, remove, then fill the cups with crushed ice and return to the freezer overnight. Make a simple syrup by bringing the sugar and water to a boil. Reduce the heat and simmer for 5 to 10 minutes, until clear and thick. While still hot, stir in a handful of mint sprigs; allow to cool. Strain the syrup into a small pitcher; discard the mint. Fifteen minutes before serving, remove the cups or glasses from the freezer. Pour 2 ounces of bourbon and 2 ounces of syrup into each ice-filled cup and decorate with a sprig of mint. Allow to sit for a few minutes, until a good coat of frost forms on the outside, and then serve. (Note: If you are using glasses, you can achieve a better frost if you wet them before placing them in the freezer the first time. Let freeze overnight. Fill with crushed ice the next day and return to the freezer for 30 minutes.) Makes 12 mint juleps.

ROOM OF A
THOUSAND MOONS

The decor in this room is the creation of architect Carlos Aparicio. The ceiling was painted by Quintin Hahn to mimic the complexity and beauty of a night sky, covered not with stars but with moons. The walls are upholstered in a cotton fabric attached with rows of evenly spaced nails. The small round table is by the French furniture maker Rulhman. The chair is by French furniture designer Leleu, circa 1930. Different-sized circles cut from Belgian wool mimic the effect of light cast on the floor surface. The early nineteenth-century table (next page) is a *table à transformation*. A felt-covered card table is revealed when the top is flipped, and the whole table can be folded into a half-moon shape and put against a wall. It is mahogany with gold-leaf bronze ornamentation on the sides. The china is Art Deco, circa 1935, "La Crémaillère" from Limoges. The glasses and silver are all nineteenth-century. The chair at the left of the table is French Empire and the chair to the right is Louis XVI.

A PALM BEACH HOSTESS

On cool days when we are fewer than ten for dinner, we eat in my small, cozy dining room," says Carol Mack. "Otherwise, we eat outside. Why be in Florida if you're going to stay inside?" Nevertheless, being inside Mack's Palm Beach house is an extraordinary experience. She sets her tables differently for each occasion, never repeating the same idea twice. Mack adores ethnic foods, and the table settings reflect the country from which the food originates. She doesn't use plain white tablecloths, maintaining that the table should reflect the hostess's taste, style, and personality. "Otherwise one might as well dine in a restaurant."

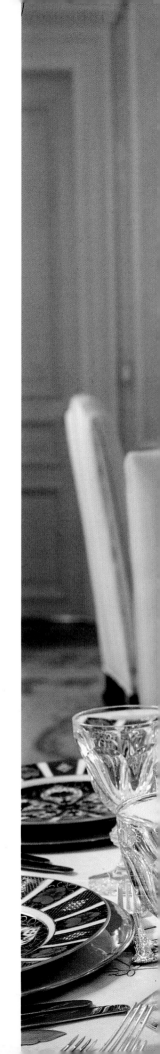

Carol Mack changes the china pattern with every course. She arranges the flowers herself, often combining them with vegetables and fruits, and uses unusual containers, such as nineteenth-century pierced ceramic bowls, different-sized cups, majolica pitchers, silver mint-julep cups, and miniature Nantucket baskets. She puts chocolate, coffee beans, nuts and crystallized ginger on the table for snacks, and uses both high and low candles—votives to make a table twinkle and higher candles to make the room glow.

Carol Mack prefers to have small lunches and large dinners. At lunch, people don't usually have enough time to mingle, and at dinner they seem to enjoy chatting with friends during cocktails and then sitting after dinner in small cozy groups for more intimate conversations. The lunches on her Palm Beach terrace are intimate occasions in an expansive setting.

LUNCH IN TOYLAND

Italian venture capitalist Jean Pigozzi spends most of his time in Europe or on his boat traveling around the world. When in New York, he lives in an eccentric pied-à-terre designed by Ettore Sottsass. Most of the furniture was also designed by Sottsass, including the four mobile tables in the center of the room. The child within the shrewd businessman is represented by the whimsical collection of antique toys and the various percussion instruments and electronic drums.

A corner of one of the Sottsass tables is cleared off for a lunch of Vietnamese spring rolls. The pearwood bar on wheels is also by Sottsass. It comes with an ice maker. On top is a sculpture made of painted wood and porcupine quills by John Goba, an artist from Sierra Leone.

LILAC TIME

Italian-born interior designer Milly de Cabrol is madly in love with New York City. She relishes night life and society, but is also a great hostess. In her old-fashioned Upper East Side apartment, she sets the Regency dining room table with Limoges plates and a collection of antique family silver. The tablecloth is a cotton Indian print. The screen is Biedermeier, the secretary is Louis XVI, and the gilded gold mirror is Baroque. Wine is served out of a decanter into thin crystal tumblers. On this occasion she has cooked a lemon rosemary chicken with roasted potatoes.

DOLLY PARTON'S LUNCH
FOR SANDY GALLIN

Dolly Parton shares an apartment in New York with producer Sandy Gallin. "In addition to enjoying my life with Sandy in general," she says, "we take vacations together all around the world. One of my favorite times was when we took my tour bus from Los Angeles to Colorado to see his brother Henry. Then we drove from Colorado to New York. This took several days, and since the bus has a fully stocked kitchen, I did lots of home cooking. Sandy ate a great deal of meat loaf." When they got to New York they ate Dolly's meat loaf and mashed potatoes in a room with a spectacular, classic New York view and entertained on white quilted cotton sofas around a Biedermeier table.

DOLLY'S MEAT LOAF

———

(Makes 5–6 servings)

1 ½ pounds ground sirloin

½ cup ketchup

½ cup tomato juice

2 eggs, beaten

¾ cup fresh bread crumbs

½ cup finely chopped onions

2 teaspoons prepared mustard

½ teaspoon salt

½ teaspoon pepper

(optional: green pepper and/or celery)

Mix all the ingredients together with your hands and put the mixture in a baking dish. Bake at 400 degrees for about 45 minutes, and then pour extra ketchup on top. Continue to bake for about 15 more minutes, or until desired doneness.

A COTTAGE IN THE HAMPTONS

The Brazilian-born interior designer Sig Bergamin has added a South American touch to an old-fashioned American cottage on Long Island. Armchairs and sofas are covered in a mixture of colorful 1950s fabrics bought in Miami. The curtains are also circa 1950. The marble table is set with Fiesta Ware pottery and plates. From the dining room window, one looks out over the garden. Outdoor dining takes place on the terrace, on a set of old French cast-iron tables and chairs.

SPICY RED SNAPPER BAHIA STYLE

———

2 tablespoons olive oil • 2 red onions, sliced
1 pound small new potatoes
2 pounds plum tomatoes, quartered
5 cloves garlic • 2 teaspoons fresh thyme • salt and pepper
3–5 pound whole red snapper, cleaned and washed
½ cup fresh coriander, chopped
3-inch piece fresh ginger, peeled and chopped
4 limes • 4 jalapeño peppers, washed and cut into 4 pieces each
2 starfruit, sliced

In a baking dish long enough for the fish, toss together the olive oil, three quarters of
the onion slices, the potatoes, tomatoes, garlic, thyme, and salt and pepper to taste.
Place the red snapper in the center of the pan, moving the mixture to the sides. Hold
the side of the fish open, sprinkle with salt and pepper, and stuff with the remaining
onion slices and the coriander and ginger. Squeeze the limes over the inside and outside of the fish. Sprinkle the top of the fish with the jalapeño peppers and the starfruit
slices. Bake at 350 degrees for approximately 1 hour.

SUMPTUOUS
COZINESS

———

Marina Palma likes to seat as many people at the table as it will allow. She sometimes uses four small tables rather than a very long one, because closeness encourages conversation. Lighting is also very important to her entertaining style. She knows that if the hostess provides all the right ingredients—good food, good wine, and an interesting mix of guests—making the evening enjoyable is an easy task for the company.

"I like my dinners to be almost sumptuous, but cozy," says Marina Palma. She has set the table here with early nineteenth-century silver and antique glasses. The tureen and porcelain plates are Royal Copenhagen's "Flora Danica" pattern.

PENNE ALLA BESCIAMELLA

———

(Serves six)

1 pound penne pasta

1 cup butter

Parmesan cheese, grated

½ pound prosciutto, very thinly sliced

1 tablespoon flour

2 cups milk

Cook the penne in lightly salted water. Drain and flavor with half the butter, a few tablespoons of Parmesan, and the prosciutto. Make the sauce by combining one quarter of the butter, the flour and the milk. It should be rather liquid. Rub the rest of the butter on the bottom and sides of an ovenproof tureen, pour in the cooked penne, and pour the warm sauce over the top. Sprinkle with grated Parmesan and place in a warm oven for a few minutes to melt the cheese.

DINNER À LA JOSEPHINE BONAPARTE

French-born collector and dealer Roger Prigent has a passion for the Imperial style. He named his business Malmaison, after the Château Malmaison, which was built at the beginning of the seventeenth century. Josephine and Napoleon lived there from 1800 to 1802, when Napoleon left for the Palais de Saint-Cloud. Josephine remained at Malmaison, which she turned into an enchanting place, accumulating collections of paintings, antiques, and plants. The gardens were scattered with greenhouses where exotic vegetation was cultivated. Napoleon gave Malmaison to Josephine at the time of their divorce in 1809. Roger Prigent has found and purchased some of the most precious objects that belonged to the emperor and the empress, and they fill the dining room here.

Roger Prigent has set an Art Deco table for a dinner in honor of Josephine. The spoons and forks are stamped with the arms of Princess Pauline Borghese, Napoleon's sister. The plates are early-nineteenth-century Sèvres porcelain. The silver candlesticks and the glasses are all early-nineteenth-century French. The Empire-period présentoir, attributed to Thomire, has been decorated with exotic fruits to evoke the gardens of Malmaison and the sugar-cane plantations of Martinique, Josephine's homeland. The big painting over the couch is a study for a large painting by Girodet, *La Révolte du Caire*, which now hangs in Versailles. The chairs around the table were made by Michel Bouvier for Napoleon's brother when he was in exile in America.

ACKNOWLEDGMENTS

Firstly, I would like to thank Olivier Gelbsmann, without whose determination and amazing eye this book would not have happened. I want to thank Sharon DeLano for her unclouded vision and for always keeping me focused on the project, Stewart O'Shields for his love of photography and his infectious drive for perfection, Yolanda Cuomo for her brilliance, Suzanne Fox for her eloquence, Mary Tantillo for her flair in organization and research, Jacqueline Coumans for her enthusiasm and for providing endless transportation, and Roger Prigent for his moral support.

Thanks to the New York shops Bardith, Ltd., The Chinese Porcelain Company, Christophe, Le Décor Français, Malmaison, and Puiforcat, and to Sam Ben Safi of Sam's Souk for their generous contributions.

And, of course, I would like to thank all of the people who so generously opened their doors, set their tables, and cooked the most delicious food. They always made us feel welcome and comfortable and we had the extreme joy, most of the time, of sitting down with them to enjoy the dishes they had so carefully prepared. I thank them from the bottom of my heart for making us feel so comfortable and making everything look so incredible: Corice Arman, Carlos Aparicio, Ann Barish, Sig Bergamin, Eric Boman and Peter Schlesinger, Muriel Brandolini, Louis Bofferding, Milly de Cabrol, Francesco Clemente, Heather Cohane, Jacqueline Coumans, Madison Cox, Frederic Fekkai, Barry Friedman and Patricia Pastor, C. Z. Guest, Susan Gutfreund, Larry Laslo, Carol Mack, Marian McEvoy, Marina Palma, Dolly Parton and Sandy Gallin, Charles Patteson, Jean Pigozzi, Roger Prigent, Katharine Rayner, Khalil Rizk, Marina Schiano, Stephen Sills and James Huniford, Jane Stubbs, and Jane Wenner.